PREPARING CRITERION-REFERENCED TESTS FOR CLASSROOM INSTRUCTION

A Title in the CURRENT TOPICS IN CLASSROOM INSTRUCTION Series

Norman E. Gronlund

Professor of Educational Psychology
University of Illinois

The Macmillan Company, New York
Collier-Macmillan Publishers, London

PRINTING   2 3 4 5 6 7 8   YEAR   5 6 7 8

Library of Congress catalog card number: 73-1041

THE MACMILLAN COMPANY
866 THIRD AVENUE, NEW YORK, NEW YORK 10022
COLLIER-MACMILLAN CANADA, LTD., TORONTO, ONTARIO

PRINTED IN THE UNITED STATES OF AMERICA

TO MY MOTHER

Preface

A fairly recent innovation in educational testing, and one that is receiving widespread attention, is that of *criterion-referenced* testing. Essentially, this technique involves an interpretation of test results in terms of the types of learning tasks students have achieved in some clearly defined area (e.g., that a student can define 90% of the terms in a science unit). Such interpretations can be most meaningfully made when the tests are intentionally designed for this purpose—that is, when they are designed to yield specific descriptions of what students can and cannot do in a particular area of learning.

This book is intended as a practical guide for the preparation and use of criterion-referenced tests in classroom instruction. The first chapter clarifies the nature of criterion-referenced testing and the principles guiding its use. Chapters 2 and 3 describe the role of criterion-referenced testing at two different levels of learning—mastery and developmental. The last three chapters describe the procedures for planning the test (Chapter 4), writing the test items (Chapter 5), and using and appraising the test (Chapter 6). The Appendix includes a check list for evaluating a criterion-referenced test and a list of useful references.

There is little theory and research to guide us in the preparation and use of criterion-referenced tests in the classroom. Thus, teacher judgment plays a prominent role in each step of test preparation. By following a systematic procedure, we can counteract some of the errors of faulty judgment but we cannot expect our judgments to be infallible. Therefore, it is essential that we consider our judgments highly tentative, and that we be willing to modify them as experience and new information make needed revision apparent.

N. E. G.

Contents

List of Tables

Chapter 1

The Nature Of Criterion-Referenced Testing

Test results can be interpreted in many different ways. A common practice with classroom tests is to list the scores in rank order and make interpretations like the following:

John's score is third from the top.
Mary's score is just average.
Henry's score is lowest in the group.

Although such interpretations clearly indicate a student's position in his classroom group, the meaningfulness of the report is dependent upon two factors that may be only vaguely known. (1) What specific learning outcomes were measured by the test? (2) What is the level of achievement of the group? Unfortunately, in all too many classrooms a student's test score signifies relative performance on a haphazard collection of test items that measure an undefined conglomerate of learning outcomes. In addition, the ability level of the group is seldom clearly defined.

The interpretation of scores on *standardized* achievement tests also typically depends on relative position in some group. Here, however, instead of a simple ranking, some type of derived score (e.g., percentile rank, standard score) is used to express relative performance. Thus, a student's test results might be reported in one of the following ways:

Bill scored at the 84th percentile rank.
Bill earned a T-score of 60.
Bill's score fell in stanine 7.

Each of these reports of Bill's test performance is indicating the same level of performance. His score fell well above average. More specifically, he surpassed 84 per cent of the students in the group. What group? In this case, the *norm* group. This is the group that took the test during the standardization process. Typically it is a carefully selected, well-defined group representing different grade or age levels on a national, regional, or state level.

The clearly defined nature of the norm group, plus the careful selection of course content, enhances the interpretation of scores from a standardized test, but note that test performance is still reported in *relative* terms. The score does not tell us specifically what the student has achieved nor how well he can perform on any given set of educational tasks. It simply tells us how high his score was in comparison to others who also took the test.

Classroom tests and standardized achievement tests that report test performance in terms of an individual's relative position in some group are called *norm-referenced* tests. Most of our present test theory and practice are based on norm-referenced testing. Basic to this measurement approach is a good spread of test scores, from high to low, so that an individual's relative standing can be more reliably determined and so that educational decisions (e.g., selection, classification, promotion) based on *differences* in performance can be made with greater confidence. This spread of test scores is also necessary for computing the common statistical measures (item analysis, reliability, validity) used in evaluating a test. The desired spread of scores is typically built-in during test construction by eliminating those items that are too easy and too difficult and by favoring items of average difficulty.

Criterion-Referenced Test Interpretation

A second method of interpreting student achievement is in terms of the type of behavior, or performance, a student is capable of demonstrating. The following statements illustrate this type of interpretation.

> Ted can add all combinations of single-digit whole numbers from 1 to 9 without error.
> Helen can spell 90% of the words in the unit word list.
> Betty can type 40 words per minute with no more than two errors.

In such interpretations a student's performance is described in behavioral (or performance) terms without reference to the level of performance of other members of the group. The level of performance that is to be accepted as satisfactory is usually predetermined and stated as part of each instructional objective, or is set for a class of objectives (e.g., mastery at 90 per cent level). Thus, the specific criterion behavior provides an absolute standard against which to compare an individual's achievement. Since a criterion standard rather than relative position in a norm group is used for describing test performance, such interpretations are called *criterion-referenced* (Glaser, 1971).

Strictly speaking, criterion-referenced measurement refers only to the method of interpreting the results and, thus, could be applied to any classroom or standardized test. This would simply involve analyzing the test, item by item, and describing each student's achievement in terms of some expected level of performance for each area of the test. Such descriptions would tend to be hazy and inadequate for most norm-referenced tests, however, for the following reasons.

1. The conglomerate of learning tasks would provide a poor frame of reference for describing individual achievement.
2. Since test items that all students answer correctly tend to be omitted from norm-referenced tests, the learning tasks mastered by the entire group would not be included in the description of an individual's achievement.
3. If multiple-choice items (or other selection type items) were used, some of the correct answers could be due to chance and the description of an individual's achievement would be distorted to an unknown degree. This is especially serious with those norm-referenced tests that use just a few test items to represent each area of achievement.

Thus, although criterion-referenced interpretations can be applied to any norm-referenced test such interpretations are fraught with pitfalls and distortions. To obtain the most meaningful and useful interpretations of this type, it is necessary to use tests that have been specifically designed for this purpose. Such tests are appropriately called *criterion-referenced tests.*

Principles of Criterion-Referenced Testing

The design and construction of criterion-referenced tests should be directed toward obtaining measures of achievement that can be expressed directly in terms of student performance on clearly specified educational tasks. Although there is a relative scarcity of theory and research to guide this process, the following principles provide a general framework within which to operate.

1. **Criterion-referenced testing requires a clearly defined and delimited domain of learning tasks.** This type of testing has been most widely and successfully used in programmed instruction, where the focus is on the mastery of a limited number of specific learning outcomes. When used with regular classroom instruction, the problem becomes one of delimiting the area to be covered by the test and of carefully defining the learning tasks in that particular achievement domain. This is easiest, of course, in the basic skill areas (e.g., arithmetic) and most difficult in such loosely structured areas as social studies. In any particular achievement area, it is also easier to define the achievement domain for the relatively simple learning outcomes (e.g., knowledge of terms) than for the more complex ones (e.g., ability to apply principles to new situations).

Part of the solution to this problem resides in dividing classroom instruction into more manageable units and constructing criterion-referenced tests for each unit. In most cases it may also be necessary to limit the use of criterion-referenced tests to measurement of the minimum essentials of the unit and to use some combination of criterion-referenced testing and norm-referenced testing for measuring achievement beyond this level.

2. **Criterion-referenced testing requires that instructional objectives be clearly defined in behavioral (performance) terms.** Since test results are to be interpreted in terms of how well a student performs on a particular set of

learning tasks, it is important that the behavior involved in the performance be clearly specified. This is typically done by stating the instructional objectives as learning outcomes. Each outcome includes a precise statement of the specific behavioral response (e.g., identifies, describes, constructs) that the student is expected to exhibit when he has attained the desired learning. As we shall see later, such statements serve as guides to test construction and aid in evaluating the adequacy of the students' test responses.

In some instances it may also be necessary, or desirable, to describe the conditions under which a particular performance is to be demonstrated (e.g., When given a paragraph of material that is new to him . . .). For most classroom tests, however, the conditions are generally understood by the students (e.g., closed book) and need not be repeated for each learning outcome.

3. Criterion-referenced testing requires that standards of performance be clearly specified. Setting appropriate standards of student performance is the key to the effective use of criterion-referenced testing in classroom instruction. It is also a major stumbling block since there is little research or theory upon which to base valid standards.

Standards of proficiency are easiest to set where they can be related to levels of performance required in out-of-school situations. The following are examples of areas where expected student performance can be described in terms of "real life" standards.

> Proficiency needed to operate an automobile.
> Proficiency required for a particular job (e.g., typing skills, laboratory skills).
> Proficiency needed to be self-sufficient in a complex society (e.g., reading a newspaper, writing a letter).

Other areas and other specific examples could, of course, be listed but even an exhaustive list would be rather limited. Most standards of school achievement must be arbitrarily set by the classroom teacher.

One solution to the problem of setting standards has been the suggestion that *mastery* should be the standard for most school learning (Carroll, 1971). This is based on the assumption that individual differences in student aptitude indicate the rate at which students learn and not the level of learning of which they are capable. Thus, all students can learn the school tasks expected of them if they are given enough time. This view of learning has caused some educators to view the terms *criterion-referenced* testing and *mastery* testing as synonymous.

Setting a standard of mastery for all, or nearly all, school tasks seems over-optimistic, in light of our current knowledge about learning. Even its most ardent advocates would agree that mastery of the more difficult and complex types of achievement would be unrealistic for many students under our present system of school instruction. Thus, at least for the present, it seems more defensible to require mastery of minimum essentials (e.g., skills basic to further learning) and to set more realistic standards of performance for learning outcomes that go beyond the minimum essentials of a course. Setting standards in this latter area is the most difficult of all. Here a teacher must rely on highly tentative standards derived largely from norm-referenced testing and from learning expectations that have been shaped and modified by his own past teaching experience. The specific problems involved will be discussed in more detail in Chapter 3.

4. **Criterion-referenced testing requires that student performance be adequately sampled within each area of performance.** Some areas of achievement are so limited that the total sample of behavior can be described and measured. This would include some lower-level learnings (counting from 1 to 10, e.g.) and some simple skills (writing the letters of the alphabet, operating a microscope, etc.). It would also include the outcomes of some training programs designed to prepare persons for relatively simple jobs. The expected learning outcomes for most classroom instruction, however, include such a wide array of specific tasks that only a limited sample of student performance can be measured in each area. In preparing a test of computational skill, for example, there are literally thousands of number combinations from which to choose. In broader and less structured areas, such as science and social studies, the number of specific tasks is almost unlimited.

The likelihood of obtaining a representative sample of student performance is enhanced (a) where the instruction is divided up into relatively small units, (b) where the domain of learning tasks is clearly defined, and (c) where specific steps are taken to obtain an adequate sample. These procedures will be elaborated upon in the following chapters.

5. **Criterion-referenced testing requires that test items be selected on the basis of how well they reflect the behavior specified in the instructional objectives.** Since criterion-referenced tests are interpreted in terms of an absolute performance standard on some clearly defined set of learning tasks, it is important that the test items be a direct measure of the expected learning outcomes. That is, the behavior called forth by each test item should match a specific behavior described in the instructional objectives. If a representative sample of such behaviors is obtained for the test, as described above, we can then generalize from test performance to the larger domain of learning tasks that the test represents.

Indirect measures of learning, such as measuring spelling skills by identifying misspelled words, are inappropriate for criterion-referenced tests. Similarly inappropriate here is selecting items on the basis of difficulty, as is done with norm-referenced tests. The difficulty of items in a criterion-referenced test should derive directly from the nature of the learning tasks measured and not from an attempt to obtain a spread of scores. In fact, where mastery is the goal, there should be little or no spread of scores since all, or nearly all, of the students should answer the items correctly.

6. **Criterion-referenced testing requires a scoring and reporting system that adequately describes student performance on clearly defined learning tasks.** A report such as the following clearly conveys what the student can do and the level of proficiency at which he can function.

The student can correctly define 90 per cent of the terms included in the unit.

The "percentage-correct" score used here is a common one in criterion-referenced testing. It is also one that has been widely used by teachers in the past. As typically used in the past, however, it indicated a percentage correct on some vaguely defined conglomerate of test items. The unique feature of criterion-referenced testing is the specific nature of the information it provides. Here, the report indicates precisely what learning tasks the student can perform at the specified level of proficiency.

It should be obvious by now that the traditional scoring systems used with norm-referenced tests (e.g., percentile ranks, standard scores) are inappropriate for criterion-referenced tests because they indicate relative position in a group.   Criterion-referenced tests are designed to describe a student's test performance in absolute terms, that is, in terms that are meaningful without reference to the performance of other students.

Criterion-Referenced Testing and Other Test Types

In addition to the major classification of tests into *norm referenced* and *criterion referenced*, there are numerous other test designations based on the particular uses of test results in teaching. Since criterion-referenced tests can be designed to serve each of the uses, it is not uncommon to confuse some of these other test types with criterion-referenced testing. Thus a brief discussion of these test types, based on instructional use, should further clarify the nature of criterion-referenced testing.

Tests are commonly used in teaching in the following ways.

1. To measure prerequisite knowledges and skills needed to begin a unit of instruction (pretest).
2. To measure progress in the development of knowledges and skills during a unit of instruction (formative test).
3. To locate learning difficulties and to clarify the nature of the difficulties during a unit of instruction (diagnostic test).
4. To measure the learning outcomes of a unit of instruction (summative test).

Each of these test types will be discussed in turn.

Pretests are, of course, criterion referenced only if they are carefully developed in accordance with the principles described earlier. A norm-referenced test can be given at the beginning of instruction, either to select those scoring highest on the test or to determine how much the students already know about the course content. Thus, although criterion-referenced pretests are very useful in teaching, all pretests are not necessarily criterion referenced.

The terms *formative* and *summative* were coined for use in curriculum evaluation (Scriven, 1967), but they are also appropriate for distinguishing among the ways that tests might be used in teaching. Formative tests are used during the instructional process to stimulate, guide, and evaluate student learning and to appraise the ongoing effectiveness of the instructional procedures. Summative tests are used at the end of instruction to determine what students have learned. As noted earlier, criterion-referenced tests can be designed to serve both of these uses. As with pretests, however, both uses can also be served by norm-referenced tests. Thus, neither of these test names should be used synonymously with criterion-referenced testing.

Diagnostic tests are designed to indicate the specific types of learning errors a student is making in a particular area of knowledge or skill. Since criterion-referenced tests provide more specific information about student learning than the traditional classroom test, they have sometimes been considered diagnostic by their very nature. The adequacy with which they serve this purpose, however, is determined by how they are constructed. Tests designed to merely indicate whether a particular standard of performance has been met may not provide detailed diagnostic information. If a student achieves 80 per cent correct in adding two-digit numbers, for example, the report does not make clear the source of his errors. Did he make errors in carrying or does he lack skill in adding certain number combinations? To answer such questions the test must be specifically designed for diagnostic use. This means focusing on the common errors of students, as well as on the criteria of successful performance, during test construction.

To summarize, although criterion-referenced testing is admirably suited to pretesting, formative testing, diagnostic testing, and summative testing, none of these terms should be used interchangeably with criterion-referenced testing.

Criterion-Referenced Testing at Different Levels of Learning

The design and construction of criterion-referenced tests present quite different problems when measuring the *mastery* of minimum essentials than when measuring student *development* beyond this minimum level. In the first case the domain of learning tasks is more limited and can be more clearly defined. This simplifies the problem of stating specific objectives, of setting standards of performance, of obtaining a representative sample of relevant test items, and of reporting student test performance. As we move beyond the mastery level, the infinite number of available learning tasks and the increased complexity of the learning outcomes pose problems that can be dealt with in only an approximate and tentative manner—at least at this stage of our knowledge. Thus, it has been decided to discuss criterion-referenced testing at two different levels. In Chapter 2 we shall describe criterion-referenced testing at the *mastery level* (i.e., learning of minimum essentials), and in Chapter 3 we shall describe criterion-referenced testing at the *developmental level* (i.e., level of excellence beyond the mastery of minimum essentials).

Criterion-Referenced Testing
And Mastery Learning

Criterion-referenced tests are easiest to design, construct, and use at the mastery level of learning. Test performance is also easiest to interpret at this level. The percentage-correct score, familiar to most teachers, provides a meaningful reporting system because it indicates how closely a student's performance approaches complete mastery on a particular learning task. The basic problem in using mastery as a goal is that of determining what specific learning outcomes students should be expected to master. This involves a review of all learning outcomes for a given course or grade level and sorting them into mastery outcomes (minimum essentials) and developmental outcomes (performance beyond the mastery of minimum essentials).

Deciding What Learning Tasks Should be Mastered

Identifying those types of achievement that are to be learned to the mastery level by all students is no simple matter and the process is somewhat arbitrary. There are two main considerations to keep in mind: (1) What *should be* mastered in a particular learning situation? (2) What *can be* mastered in a particular learning situation? Answers to the first question can be guided by considerations such as the following:

1. What minimum knowledge and skills are prerequisite to further learning in the same area (e.g., knowledge of terms, measurement skills)?
2. What basic skills are prerequisite to learning in other areas (e.g., reading skills, computational skills, language skills)?
3. What minimum skill is needed for safe performance in some particular activity (e.g., using laboratory equipment, driving an automobile)?
4. What knowledge and skills are needed to attain minimum job proficiency (e.g., lathe operation, typing skill)?
5. What minimum knowledge and skills are needed to function in everyday, out-of-school, situations (e.g., reading, writing, speaking)?

These and similar questions should help clarify what learning outcomes we might expect students to master in a particular area of instruction at a given grade level. The main point is that explicit criteria are needed in identifying those situations where mastery is necessary or desirable. Mastery of particular learning tasks should have some significance beyond the fact that a teacher has arbitrarily set mastery as the goal.

Whether or not students *can* efficiently master the learning tasks at a particular level of instruction is equally important in selecting outcomes for mastery learning. Here we must consider the age level of the students, the ability level of the particular group, and the past learning experiences of the students. Although the concept of "learning readiness" has been challenged by the shifting of difficult learning tasks to the elementary grades (e.g., mathematics and foreign language study), readiness is still an important consideration. When students are required to learn tasks for which they are not fully ready, an inordinate amount of time is apt to be needed to achieve mastery. As a consequence, achievement in other areas is likely to suffer. Note, for example, the usual decline in computational skill when modern mathematics is introduced at the elementary school level.

Whenever possible, it is desirable to have the identification of the mastery level outcomes done cooperatively by all of the teachers in the school. If some consensus can be arrived at concerning what these learning outcomes should be and at what grade level they should be taught, a more sequential arrangement of learning tasks can be obtained. This would also make it easier to identify the minimum skills needed to move smoothly from one learning stage to another.

Teachers should, of course, not depend entirely on their own resources in determining what learning tasks should be mastered at a given level. The recommendations of subject-matter authorities, curriculum experts, and learning specialists should also be considered.

Delimiting the Area to Be Tested

As noted earlier, one way to limit the area to be tested by a criterion-referenced test is to divide the course, or learning domain, into relatively small units. These should be coherent units based on some clearly defined topic of some other meaningful segment of instruction. Units of a week or two have been found to be especially useful (Block, 1971).

Developing criterion-referenced tests for each instructional unit may involve more testing than is typically done by teachers, but more frequent testing of this type has special advantages. Since achievement is reported in terms of the specific learning tasks that each student has and has not mastered, the results are directly useful in instruction. They indicate to both the student and the teacher the areas of learning where further attention is needed. If constructed with diagnosis in mind, they can also reveal the sources of learning difficulty and suggest the types of remedial work that might be most beneficial.

Limiting the area of achievement to be covered by a criterion-referenced test is important for reasons beyond its utility as an instructional aid. With this type of testing there is always a problem of maintaining reasonable test length because of the specific nature of the measurement. To maintain satisfactory reliability it is necessary to have a number of test items for each specific learning task. Thus, where there is a relatively large number of learning tasks, the length of the test soon becomes unmanageable. Testing by units keeps the specific learning tasks within a reasonable number and the test to a practicable size.

Defining the Learning Outcomes

The general procedure for defining instructional objectives in terms of specific learning outcomes has been described in detail elsewhere (Gronlund, 1970, 1971). Here we shall simply outline and illustrate the procedure to clarify its role in preparing criterion-referenced tests.

In preparing objectives for classroom instruction it is usually desirable to follow a two-step process. First, the instructional objectives are stated as general learning outcomes. Second, each instructional objective is further defined by listing the specific learning tasks on which students are to demonstrate performance at the end of the learning experience to show that they have achieved the instructional objective. This procedure results in statements of learning outcomes like the following:

Knows the meaning of basic terms of the unit
1. Writes a definition of the term.
2. States one alternate meaning of the term.
3. Distinguishes between terms that are similar in meaning.
4. Identifies a synonym of the term.
5. Identifies an antonym of the term.
6. Matches a term to a picture of the concept.
7. Identifies the meaning of the term when used in a sentence.

This, of course, is not an exhaustive list but it illustrates the process of defining instructional objectives in terms of specific learning outcomes. Note that the verb in the general instructional objective is not stated in behavioral or performance terms. Instead, the verb *knows* indicates a class of specific learning outcomes in which we are interested. Using a general instructional objective, such as this, helps retain the unity of instruction and prevents us from focusing on a collection of isolated and unrelated learning tasks. It also makes it possible to report student achievement in terms of both the specific learning outcomes (writes a definition) and the larger domain of behavior the specific tasks represent (knows the meaning of terms).

The specific learning outcomes, or learning tasks, listed beneath each general instructional objective should begin with an action verb that indictates specific observable behavior. These are called *behavioral* or *per-*

formance terms because they describe the precise type of behavior, or performance, to be demonstrated by the student as evidence of his achievement of the learning task.   The following action verbs from the preceding list of specific learning outcomes are listed to clarify the nature of behavioral terms:

> Writes.
> States.
> Distinguishes between.
> Identifies.
> Matches.

Terms such as these provide definite guidelines for both teaching and testing. How do you determine whether a student can *write* a definition of a term? Simply ask him to write one.   Thus, when the instructional objectives are defined in such specific behavioral terms, the test items can be directly related to the learning outcomes to be measured.   The specific learning outcomes describe the desired student behavior and the test items present tasks that call forth that particular behavior.

Where the test is to be used primarily for diagnostic purposes, as in the basic skill area, the learning outcomes must be analyzed in even greater detail.   Such a specific outcome as "adds whole numbers," for example, might be further analyzed into specific tasks like the following:

> 1.   Adds two single-digit numbers with sums of ten or less (2 + 5).
> 2.   Adds two single-digit numbers with sums greater than ten (6 + 8).
> 3.   Adds three single digit numbers with sums of ten or less (2 + 4 + 3).
> 4.   Adds three single-digit numbers with sums greater than ten (7 + 5 + 9).
> 5.   Adds two two-digit numbers without carrying (21 + 34).
> 6.   Adds two two-digit numbers with simple carrying (36 + 27).
> 7.   Adds two two-digit numbers with carrying into 9 (57 + 48).
> 8.   Adds two or more three-digit numbers with repeated carrying (687 + 839).

The problems in the parentheses are merely intended as illustrations of each of the tasks.   Typically, the numbers would be arranged in columns, although in some instances it might be desirable to present them both ways. In addition, each of the tasks would be tested by a number of items to provide an adequate sample of performance.   This illustrates the point that was made earlier concerning the need to delimit the area to be measured in order to keep test length within reasonable bounds.   Note, for example, that if we were to include only five problems for each of the tasks, we would have a test of forty items.   A diagnostic test at this level of detail for all types of computation with whole numbers (addition, subtraction, division, and multiplication) would require 160 items.   Thus, with greater specificity in the analysis of the learning tasks, comprehensive coverage can be obtained only by delimiting the area to be tested and by testing more frequently.

Setting Standards of Performance

As noted earlier, standards of performance can be set for each specific learning outcome or for each general instructional objective. It is usually desirable to set standards for each specific task when performance is expressed in terms of the time required to complete the task (e.g., locates a malfunction in a TV set in 15 minutes), the precision with which the task is performed (e.g., measures the length of a board within one-eighth of an inch), or the number of errors that are allowed (e.g., takes dictation at a normal speaking rate with no more than two errors per page). Such situations are relatively rare in classroom testing, however, so it is usually possible to set one standard of performance for each general instructional objective. For mastery tests, the standard is typically expressed in terms of the percentage of test items that the student is expected to answer correctly.

At first glance, 100 per cent mastery might seem to be the ideal criterion for a mastery test. However, the work of Block (1971) has suggested that 80 to 85 per cent correct is a more realistic standard. He noted that setting the standard too high may be wasteful of teacher and student time, and may have a negative effect on student motivation. The lower standard tends to provide more opportunities for student success and thus increases the amount of positive reinforcement.

Since there is little empirical evidence to support any given level of mastery in classroom instruction, the best we can do is arbitrarily set a standard and then adjust it up or down as experience dictates. The following steps illustrate this approach.

1. Lacking other evidence, start by arbitrarily setting the level of mastery for each item type as follows:

Short-answer	80% correct
Multiple-choice	85% correct
True-false	90% correct

   The different "percentages correct" take into account the fact that you can get a certain percentage of the items correct on a true-false test (50%) and a multiple choice test (25%) by guessing alone.

2. If a higher level of mastery is necessary for effective learning at the next stage of instruction, increase the required "percentage correct." For simple computational skills, for example, complete mastery might be set as the goal.

3. If a higher level of mastery is necessary for safe performance in some activity, increase the required "percentage correct." Before a student is permitted to operate dangerous laboratory or shop equipment, for example, complete mastery of the procedure and of the safety precautions might be required.

4. If a test, or subtest, is relatively short, increase the required "percentage correct." This allows for the smaller, and thus less dependable, sample of behavior.

5. If experience in teaching the material indicates that a higher or lower level of mastery is desirable, adjust the "percentage correct" as indicated. The objectives for an instructional unit may be easier or more difficult to attain than was originally anticipated, for example. Or, it may be found that because of repetition of the knowledge and skills in the next unit of study, a high level of mastery at the initial stages of instruction is unnecessary.

In final analysis, the important question is, *What level of mastery is necessary in order to learn effectively at the next stage of instruction?* Unfortunately, there are few answers to this question. Until further evidence is available, we need to depend largely on judgments based on our own teaching experience. Hopefully a systematic approach such as that described above will increase the likelihood of setting more satisfactory standards of performance.

Obtaining a Representative Sample of Behavior

A basic problem with criterion-referenced testing is that of obtaining a representative sample of the student performance we wish to describe. We may, for example, want to determine how well a student can spell the words in a 200-item word list. Since a 200-item spelling test would be impractical, we need to obtain a sample of words from this list in such a way that student performance on the shorter list of words (sample) would represent his performance on the longer list (larger domain of behavior). In this case we could simply arrange the words in alphabetical order and select every tenth word. This would give us a 20-item spelling test that was representative of the larger domain of behavior in which we were interested. If a student could spell 90 per cent of these 20 words, we would then be willing to say that he could probably spell 90 per cent of the words in the longer list. Thus, we could generalize from our test results to the larger domain of behavior that the sample represented.

A test is almost always a *sample* of tasks that was selected to represent some larger domain of behavior. If we are to generalzie from the specific tasks in the test (e.g., 7 + 6 + 9) to the larger domain of behavior (e.g., adds whole numbers), then we must have some assurance that the sample of tasks is truly representative. This is easiest to do in the basic skill areas and becomes increasingly difficult as we move to the less clearly structured content areas.

Representative sampling is enhanced if the two steps described earlier have been completed. That is, (1) the area to be tested has been delimited to a relatively small unit of instruction, and (2) the learning outcomes to be measured have been clearly defined. For most testing situations, the next step should be the preparation of a table of specifications. This is a twofold table that lists the learning outcomes across the top and the areas of content down the side. Each cell in the table can then be used to specify the number of test items needed for adequate sampling of the larger domain of behavior that the table represents. An example of such a table is shown in Table I.

TABLE I. Table of Specifications for a 40-Item Test on Addition of Fractions

Content Area \ Instructional Objectives	Adds Fractions	Adds Fractions and Mixed Numbers	Adds Mixed Numbers	Total Items
Denominators are alike	5	4	4	13
Denominators are unlike (with common factor)	5	4	4	13
Denominators are unlike (without common factor)	6	4	4	14
Total items	16	12	12	40

It will be noted in our illustrative table that sixteen test items will measure the addition of fractions with fractions. Of these, five problems will have like denominators (1/4 + 2/4 = 3/4), five will have unlike denominators *with* a common factor (1/4 + 1/8 = 3/8), and six will have unlike denominators *without* a common factor (1/4 + 1/3 = 7/12). The other columns are read in a similar manner.

The number of test items in each cell of a table of specifications should, of course, reflect the instructional emphasis of the unit. In addition, enough test items should be included to fit the types of interpretations we wish to make. As a rule of thumb, it would be desirable to have at least several test items for each specific type of performance to be described and ten or more items for each general instructional objective. The larger the number of items we use for each specific learning outcome, the more dependable the results and the more useful they will be for diagnostic purposes.

Preparing Criterion-Referenced Test Items

When the learning outcomes have been clearly specified and the sample to be measured has been explicitly defined, the preparation of relevant test items is ready to begin. The specific nature of the test items to be used should be determined largely by the performance tasks stated in the specific learning outcomes. If, for example, the task is one of *computing, naming,* or *describing* then an item type that requires the student to supply the answer is indicated. If the task calls for *identifying* a correct answer or statement, then items calling for the selection of the correct answer would be appropriate. In criterion-referenced testing, each learning outcome should be measured as directly as possible since performance on the test tasks is used to describe precisely what the student can do.

As noted earlier, a basic difference between criterion-referenced tests and norm-referenced tests resides in the difficulty of the test items. In norm-referenced tests the items are deliberately designed to obtain a large spread of scores so that students can be reliably ranked in order of achievement. In criterion-referenced mastery tests, however, a spread of scores is neither expected nor desired. The difficulty of the test items should be derived directly from the learning tasks to be measured. If none of the students (or only a few) can answer an item before instruction but all of them can answer it after instruction, both the test item and the instruction have been effective. Thus, for criterion-referenced tests at the mastery level, the *ideal* would be a zero spread of scores at the end of instruction. That is, all students would have demonstrated complete mastery by obtaining correct answers to all items. This ideal is, of course, seldom obtained but it highlights the fact that variation in test scores is not relevant to such testing.

The above discussion should not be interpreted to mean that item difficulty can be ignored when constructing criterion-referenced mastery tests. On the contrary, special care must be taken to match the difficulty of the test task to the difficulty of the performance task described in the specific learning outcome. The test task should be neither easier nor more difficult. Obtaining a specified level of item difficulty also requires special precautions during item writing. Here, one must avoid introducing irrelevant clues to the answer, irrelevant sources of difficulty (e.g., ambiguity), or any other factor that might alter the student's response to the test task. In the final analysis, we want test performance to be a valid indicator of the presence or absence of the specific behaviors defined in the expected learning outcomes.

Step-by-step procedures for planning a criterion-referenced mastery test are presented in Chapter 4 and specific suggestions for writing the test items are presented in Chapter 5.

Chapter 3

Criterion-Referenced Testing And Developmental Learning

Criterion-referenced testing is most useful at the *mastery* level of learning, for the following reasons:

1. The learning outcomes are relatively simple (knowledge and basic skills).
2. The domain of behavior is rather limited (minimum essentials).
3. The learning is frequently sequential in nature (arithmetic).
4. The percentage-correct score provides a meaningful report (indicates degree of progress toward complete mastery).

These conditions make it possible to more clearly define the domain of behavior to be tested, to more adequately sample the learning tasks to be included in the test, and to more easily set criterion standards for judging and reporting student performance.

The difficulty of using criterion-referenced tests at the *developmental* level (i.e., learning beyond the minimum essentials) results to a large extent from the fact that at this level none of the above conditions exist. Instead, the learning outcomes are complex (e.g., understanding, thinking skills), the domain of learning tasks is virtually unlimited, and the learning seldom proceeds through a neat sequence of stages. In addition, the instructional objectives represent goals to work toward rather than goals to be fully achieved, for here the emphasis is on the continuous development of understanding and skill. Each student is encouraged to strive for the maximum level of achievement and excellence of which he is capable, rather than the mastery of some predetermined set of minimum essentials. Under such conditions the meaning of the percentage-correct score is rather ambiguous.

The lack of structure and clearly defined limits at the developmental level of learning places severe restrictions on the use of criterion-referenced tests. At this level it is necessary to resort to norm-referenced testing. If these tests are carefully developed along lines similar to those of criterion-referenced mastery tests, however, it is possible to make some criterion-referenced interpretations of the test scores. Although such interpretations will not be as precise as those at the mastery level, they will provide a useful adjunct to the interpretations based on the relative ranking of students.

Types of Instructional Objectives at the Developmental Level

While learning at the mastery level is concerned primarily with simple knowledge outcomes (e.g., knowledge of terms) and basic skills (e.g., computation, grammar) learning at the developmental level is concerned with complex types of achievement.   That is, achievement that goes beyond the simple remembering of learned material or the repetition of previously learned skills. Complex types of achievement typically demand some novelty in the student's response. They also frequently require the integration of ideas and responses into patterns of behavior that are more than a sum of the series of specific responses involved. We can identify and separately measure many of the specific skills involved in reading, for example, but reading comprehension is more than an accumulation of these specific skills. It is an integrated response pattern that must be measured as a total functioning unit.   Thus, although we can teach and test some specific reading skills (e.g., word-attack skills) at the mastery level, reading comprehension is a complex, continuously developing process that cannot be reduced to the mastery of specific skills.

The following instructional objectives illustrate the nature of learning outcomes at the developmental level.

> Understands concepts and principles.
> Applies concepts and principles to new situations.
> Uses a scientific approach in solving problems.
> Demonstrates mathematical reasoning ability.
> Writes a creative short story.
> Demonstrates critical thinking skills.
> Evaluates the adequacy of a given experiment.
> Performs skillfully on a musical instrument.

As noted earlier, students cannot be expected to fully achieve such objectives. Even the simplest of these (understands concepts and principles) is a matter of degree and can be continuously developed throughout life. All we can reasonably expect to do for a particular course or unit of instruction is to identify a sample of specific learning outcomes that represent degrees of progress toward the objectives. It would be impossible to identify all specific behaviors involved in such complex patterns of response. Even if we could, the measurement of each specific behavior would not be the same as measuring the integrated response pattern. Thus, we need to focus on the types of student performance that are most indicative of progress toward the objectives at that particular level of instruction.

Delimiting the Area to Be Tested

Here, as with mastery testing, it is desirable to restrict the area to be tested wherever possible. Except for final examinations, tests should be confined to relatively limited instructional units. This will make it possible to measure a more adequate sample of behavior without extending testing time beyond a single class period. The adequacy of the sampling for the final examination can be allowed for by constructing longer tests and by extending the testing time for the final examination to several class periods.

Defining the Learning Outcomes

The procedure for defining instructional objectives in behavioral terms at the developmental level is the same as that used at the mastery level. The major difference lies in the proportion of specific learning outcomes that can be listed for a given objective. At the mastery level the domain of behavior is typically so restricted (e.g., adds whole numbers) that a relatively large   proportion of the specific learning tasks can be identified. At the developmental level, however, such a vast array of specific outcomes is possible that only a limited sample of them can be listed for each objective. Thus, special attention must be directed toward listing those learning outcomes that best represent the attainment of the objective. What we want is a list that is comprehensive enough to describe what students are like who have achieved the objective and yet brief enough to be easily manageable. The following objective and list of specific learning outcomes illustrates an adequate degree of specificity for defining outcomes at the developmental level (see Gronlund, 1970, for other examples).

Understands scientific principles

1. States the principle in his own words.
2. Identifies an example of the principle.
3. Identifies the relationship between two principles.
4. Predicts an outcome based on the principle.
5. Formulates hypotheses in harmony with the principle.
6. Distinguishes between correct and incorrect applications of the principle.

Although other specific learning outcomes could be listed for this objective, the above six provide a fairly clear description of what is meant by "understanding scientific principles." We assume that how a student performs on these particular tasks indicates how he would probably perform on the other tasks, representing the same general objective.

The adequacy of the list of specific learning outcomes for each objective can be determined by asking the following questions:

1. Is each specific outcome stated in *behavioral* terms?
2. Is each specific outcome *relevant* to the objective?
3. Do the specific outcomes provide a representative sample of the behavior encompassed by the objective?

Answers to these questions depend largely on personal judgment but they serve to focus attention on the criteria to consider when evaluating the final list.

Obtaining a Representative Sample of Behavior

If we are to report student achievement at the developmental level in terms of performance on a particular set of learning tasks, as well as relative position in some group, special care must be taken to obtain a representative sample of student performance. This is the same problem encountered at the mastery level, of course, but here the task is much more complex. At this level we have three factors that increase the difficulty of obtaining an adequate sample. (1) It is impossible to fully define the domain of expected achievement in a particular area. (2) We can only measure a very limited sample of the many specific performance tasks assumed to be included in a particular area. (3) We can only measure degrees of progress toward the objectives, rather than complete mastery.

One method of coping with the above difficulties is to make each objective the focal point of test construction and test interpretation. This means including in the table of specifications a more detailed breakdown for each general objective, constructing a set of test items that adequately samples all specific outcomes that have been listed for an objective, including test items that range from easy to difficult for each objective, and describing student test performance by objective rather than by total test score only. Focusing our testing procedures on each objective increases the likelihood of an adequate sample of behavior and makes possible more explicit statements concerning the types of tasks a student can or cannot perform. Although these descriptions may not be as definitive as those at the mastery level, they provide a good supplement to test interpretations based on the student's relative position in some group.

The amount of detail to include in a table of specifications at the developmental level depends to a large extent on how broad the area is that the test is to cover. If the test is to be designed for a rather limited area of achievement at the end of a unit, it may be desirable to include in the table all specific learning outcomes that have been listed for each objective. For a broader area, such as that shown in Table II, it may be necessary to limit the breakdown to the major areas of content and the general instructional objectives.

Each objective listed in Table II (e.g., understands principles) would, of course, be defined by a list of specific learning outcomes, as illustrated earlier, but they need not be included in the table. They would be used during test construction, however, and test items should be developed for each specific outcome.

Note that by designing a test to fit Table II and grouping the items within the test by objective, we can make interpretations that would otherwise not be possible. We might, for example, report that a student has a good "understanding of terms, facts, and concepts" but is weak on "understanding of principles and procedures." A more detailed report could be obtained by analyzing student performance on each of the specific learning outcomes. Thus, we might note that a student can "state a principle in his own words" but he can't "identify an example of the principle" or "predict an outcome based on the principle." These latter, more specific, interpretations are, of course, more useful for instructional purposes.

TABLE II. Table of Specifications for a 100-Item Test
of Understanding in General Science

Instructional Objectives / Content Areas	Understanding of					Total Items
	Terms	Facts	Concepts	Principles	Procedures	
Biology	5	5	6	7	7	30
Chemistry	4	3	4	5	4	20
Physics	3	3	3	3	3	15
Astronomy	3	3	3	3	3	15
Earth Science	3	4	4	4	5	20
Total Items	18	18	20	22	22	100

Setting Standards of Performance

Setting standards of performance at the developmental level is extremely hazardous since there are so few guidelines to follow. Here, we expect students to show continuous development, so complete mastery is not an appropriate standard. How much progress students can be expected to achieve toward particular objectives depends on the age level of the students, the learning ability of the students, the effectiveness of the instruction, and the difficulty of the test items. It would be impossible to make very precise judgments concerning expected levels of performance under these conditions. What we do in practice is to set general levels of expectation, to teach and test at these levels, and then to refine our judgments concerning the expected levels of performance on the basis of our experience.

The lack of a clear set of standards for evaluating test performance at the developmental level means we must depend largely on norm-referenced interpretations. That is, on the relative position a student holds in a particular group. It doesn't mean, however, that we must depend on norm-referenced interpretations alone. If the test is carefully developed along the lines described earlier, we can then supplement norm-referenced interpretations with descriptions of the types of learning tasks the student can perform. Thus, test performance can be described in terms of both what the student can do (e.g., interpret graphs) and how his performance compares to others in his group (e.g., 70 per cent of the students did less well). By combining the two types of interpretation we can provide more adequate descriptions of student learning. Hopefully this procedure will also further clarify expected student performance on each objective so that more adequate standards of performance can be set for future groups. As experience is obtained in a particular area of instruction, it may be possible to eventually set nonmastery performance standards in terms of percentage correct (e.g., 60 per cent correct) that are both reasonable and feasible for each instructional objective.

Preparing Test Items

The preparation of test items at the developmental level follows the same procedure as that at the mastery level. The objectives are defined in terms of specific learning outcomes, the content is outlined, a table of specifications is built, and then test items are written to fit the table of specifications. Each test item is designed to call forth the specific behavior described by one of the specific learning outcomes. This procedure is described and illustrated in Chapters 4 and 5 and in other references on testing (Gronlund 1968, 1970, 1971).

A major difference in test construction at the mastery and developmental levels has to do with the difficulty of the test items. As noted earlier, the difficulty of the items in a criterion-referenced mastery test is determined by the nature of the learning tasks to be mastered. If the tasks are simple, the test items are simple. If the tasks are of moderate difficulty, the test items are of moderate difficulty. No attempt is made to obtain a spread of scores based on difficulty. On a criterion-referenced mastery test, we expect all students to obtain perfect, or near perfect, scores when the instruction has been effective. On a test at the developmental level, however, we need test items of varying difficulty for each objective. Here, where complete mastery is not possible, we need a range of item difficulty in order to report a student's relative degree of progress toward each objective (criterion-referenced interpretation) and his relative position in some clearly defined group (norm-referenced interpretation).

If the specific learning outcomes for each objective cover a range of difficulty, it may be a simple matter of matching the items to the behavior described in the outcomes. The specific outcomes listed below for reading comprehension, for example, illustrate tasks of increasing difficulty.

> Identifies *details* that are explicitly stated in a passage.
> Identifies the *main thought* of a passage.
> Identifies *inferences* drawn from a passage.

It is not always possible to have such a neat ordering of specific learning outcomes in terms of level of difficulty. In some content areas the specific outcomes may be of approximately equal difficulty for a given objective. In such cases a range of item difficulty is obtained by considering the difficulty of the instructional content toward which the student is to respond. Thus, he may be asked to demonstrate understanding of increasingly complex concepts and principles, or applications to increasingly difficult problems.

At the developmental level, we are interested in each student learning as much as he can beyond the minimum essentials of the course. Thus, a wide range of difficulty is needed to adequately describe student performance. Except for a few easy items at the beginning of the test for motivational purposes, the items should range from the 95 per cent level of difficulty (95 per cent correct) to the 5 per cent level of difficulty (5 per cent correct). This will enable each student to demonstrate the level of performance he has achieved beyond the mastery of minimum essentials.

In obtaining a range of item difficulty, one should not attempt to increase difficulty by using obscure material, by calling for discriminations that are educationally unimportant, or by any other means that makes the test a less valid measure of the learning outcomes. The difficulty of the items should result directly from the complexity of the subject-matter content included in the instruction and from the type of reaction students are expected to make to that content (e.g., understanding, application).

Summary Comparison of Testing at the Mastery and Developmental Levels

Criterion-referenced testing is most useful in classroom instruction where the learning outcomes are relatively simple and mastery provides a realistic standard of performance. Where the learning outcomes are complex and each student is encouraged to achieve the maximum level of performance of which he is capable, some modification in testing procedure is necessary. At present, the best means of measuring student development toward these goals beyond mastery is that of constructing norm-referenced tests that can also provide some criterion-referenced interpretations of student performance.

The similarities and differences between criterion-referenced mastery testing and testing at the developmental level are summarized in Table III.

For most classroom instruction it is desirable to construct both types of tests. The criterion-referenced mastery test will indicate the extent to which the minimum standards of the course are being met and the test at the developmental level will indicate the degree to which students are progressing beyond these minimum standards. In some cases it may be desirable to include both types of measurement in a single classroom test. When this is done the mastery items should be placed first, in a separate part, and both parts should have the items grouped by objective for ease of interpretation.

TABLE III. Summary Comparison of Criterion-Referenced Mastery Testing and Testing at the Developmental Level

	Criterion-Referenced Mastery Testing	Testing at the Developmental Level
Purpose	Measure mastery of minimum essentials.	Measure degree of achievement beyond the mastery of minimum essentials.
Types of Learning Tasks	Basic skills and simple knowledge outcomes that are prerequisite to further learning. Minimum skills needed to perform some important task safely and effectively.	Complex types of achievement that depend on an integrated response pattern that typically must be measured as a total functioning unit (understanding, application, thinking skills).

TABLE III. Summary Comparison of Criterion-Referenced Mastery Testing
and Testing at the Developmental Level (cont'd)

	Criterion-Referenced Mastery-Testing	*Testing at the Developmental Level*
Nature of the Learning	Learning is frequently sequential. Specific tasks can be learned separately and in a clearly defined sequence.	Learning is seldom sequential. Complex learning outcomes depend on the cumulative effect of many diverse learning experiences that can be organized and integrated in many different ways.
Nature of the Instructional Objectives	Objectives are limited to instructional outcomes that can be fully mastered.	Objectives provide direction toward goals that can never be fully achieved.
Specifying the Specific Learning Outcomes	Limited domain of behavior makes it possible to clearly define the domain. A relatively large proportion of the specific learning outcomes can be identified for each objective.	Unlimited domain of behavior makes complete definition impossible. Only a relatively small proportion of the specific learning outcomes can be identified for each objective.
Building the Table of Specifications	Confine to a unit of instruction and include all, or nearly all, learning outcomes and content areas to be measured.	Confine to some clearly defined area of instruction and include a representative sample of the learning outcomes and content areas to be measured.
Setting Performance Standards	Arbitrarily set level of mastery at 85% correct and adjust up or down as experience dictates.	Use norm-referenced interpretations and develop approximate nonmastery standards from experience in teaching and testing.
Constructing Test Items	Match item difficulty to the difficulty of the learning task to be measured and follow standard rules of item construction	Obtain range of item difficulty for each objective and follow standard rules of item construction.
Reporting Test Results	Indicate degree of mastery of each objective, or unit of instruction, by using percentage-correct score, and classify performances as mastery or nonmastery.	Indicate relative degree of progress toward each objective by describing performance (or using percentage-correct score), and indicate relative level of performance by indicating position in some clearly defined group.

Chapter 4
Steps In Planning The Test

Planning for a classroom test follows essentially the same steps, whether we are preparing a criterion-referenced mastery test or a norm-referenced test designed to yield some criterion-referenced interpretations. Thus, in this chapter we shall describe the steps one-by-one, using a unit on "weather maps" in elementary science to illustrate the process. Although this unit is to be taught at the mastery level, comments concerning needed variations for testing at the developmental level will be included where appropriate.

Delimit the Area to Be Tested

The first step in planning for a classroom test is to delimit the achievement area to a reasonable size unit of instruction. A unit covering a week or two is probably most desirable. Our illustrative unit on "weather maps" was designed to cover a two-week period in elementary science.

Final examinations designed to cover a semester of work must, of course, sample from a much broader area of instruction. If plans for unit tests have been carefully developed throughout the semester, however, they can aid in preparing a final examination that adequately samples from all units of instruction.

State the Objectives and Define Them in Specific Terms

The general instructional objectives are usually stated first. Each instructional objective is then further defined by listing a representative sample of the specific types of behavior students are to demonstrate at the end of the unit. This procedure is described in detail, using a variety of illustrations from different teaching areas, in an earlier publication (Gronlund, 1970).

The following list of general instructional objectives and specific learning outcomes was developed for our unit on "weather maps." Although the list is not exhaustive, it illustrates the procedure for stating the objectives and it indicates the desired amount of detail.

Objectives for a Unit on Weather Maps

1. Knows basic terms.
    1.1 Writes a definition of each term.
    1.2 Identifies the term that represents each weather element.
    1.3 Identifies the term that best fits a given weather description.
    1.4 Matches the term to a picture of the concept.
    1.5 Distinguishes between correct and incorrect uses of the term.

2. Knows map symbols.
    2.1. Matches each symbol with the name of the weather element it represents.
    2.2 Draws the symbol for each weather element.
    2.3 Identifies the meaning of each symbol shown on a weather map.

3. Knows specific facts.
    3.1 Lists the characteristics of a given weather condition.
    3.2 Identifies the elements affecting a given weather condition.
    3.3 Names the instrument used for measuring each weather element.
    3.4 Identifies the unit of measurement used in reporting each weather element on a weather map.
    3.5 Distinguishes between correct and incorrect procedures for determining each weather element.
    3.6 Matches the names of each cloud type with a description of its characteristics.
    3.7 Identifies the weather conditions associated with each type of front.

4. Interprets weather maps.
    4.1 Describes the weather for a given locality.
    4.2 Identifies the different types of fronts shown on a weather map.
    4.3 Describes the weather conditions surrounding each front shown on a weather map.
    4.4 Identifies the direction of movement for each front shown on a weather map.

It will be noted that this list of objectives is limited to simple knowledge outcomes and to simple interpretive skills that can be measured by a mastery test. It does not include learning outcomes at the developmental level (e.g., understands scientific principles underlying atmospheric conditions), nor does it include performance skills (e.g., constructs weather maps) or affective outcomes (e.g., demonstrates scientific attitude). A more elaborate evaluation plan for a weather unit might contain a listing of all relevant objectives with an indication of how each objective is to be evaluated. Here we are focusing on the preparation of a criterion-referenced mastery test and have limited our list of objectives accordingly.

Make a Content Outline

The list of objectives and specific learning outcomes describe the types of behavioral responses students are expected to make (e.g., defines terms) and the course content indicates the subject-matter topics toward which the students are expected to respond (e.g., air pressure). Thus, a content outline also should be included in the test plan. The amount of detail to be included in the content outline is somewhat arbitrary, but it should be detailed enough to assure that the test contains an adequate sample of the content included in the instruction. The following list of subject-matter topics for our unit on "weather maps" illustrates an adequate outline for test planning.

Content Outline for a Unit on Weather Maps

A. Air pressure
1. Measuring and reporting air pressure.
2. Factors affecting air pressure.
3. Relation to weather changes.
B. Air temperature
1. Measuring and reporting air temperature.
2. Factors affecting air temperature.
3. Relation to weather formations.
C. Humidity and Precipitation
1. Measuring and reporting humidity.
2. Factors affecting humidity.
3. Forms of precipitation.
4. Measuring and reporting precipitation.
D. Wind
1. Measurement of speed and direction.
2. Factors affecting speed and direction.
3. Symbols for reporting speed and directions.
E. Clouds
1. Types of clouds.
2. Characteristics of cloud types.
3. Factors causing cloud formations.
4. Relation to weather conditions.
5. Symbols for cloud types.
F. Fronts
1. Types of fronts.
2. Formation of fronts.
3. Weather related to fronts.
4. Symbols for fronts.

For instructional purposes some teachers prefer to expand the above outline to include all terms, symbols, and specific facts that the students are expected to master. Where this is done, the more elaborate outline used for instruction may, of course, also be used for testing purposes.

Prepare a Table of Specifications

The use of a table of specifications provides greater assurance that our test will measure a representative sample of the instructional objectives and the

TABLE IV. Table of Specifications for a 60-Item Test on Weather Maps

Instructional Objectives / *Content Areas*	*1.* *Knows Basic Terms*	*2.* *Knows Map Symbols*	*3.* *Knows Specific Facts*	*4.* *Interprets Weather Maps*	*Total Items*
A. Air pressure	2	2	2	2	8
B. Air temperature	2	2	2	2	8
C. Humidity and precipitation	2	2	3	3	10
D. Wind	2	3	3	4	12
E. Clouds	3	2	3	2	10
F. Fronts	3	3	3	3	12
Total Items	14	14	16	16	60

content included in the instruction. The instructional objectives are typically listed across the top of the table and the content areas are listed down the left side. Each objective and each area of content are then weighted in terms of their relative importance (e.g., amount of instructional time used), and numbers are placed in the cells to indicate the number of test items to be allotted to each objective and each area of content.

A table of specifications for our unit on "weather maps" is presented in Table IV. Note that fourteen items are to be constructed for the first objective, *Knows Basic Terms*. Of these, two will be on "air pressure," two on "air temperature," two on "humidity and precipitation," two on "wind," three on "clouds." and three on "fronts." The remainder of the table is read in the same manner. Since many of the specific learning outcomes are measured by only two test items, our test interpretation will need to be confined to student performance on the general instructional objectives.

Only the general instructional objectives and the general areas of content were included in Table IV. A more detailed test plan can be obtained by including all specific learning outcomes and all subject-matter topics. This latter procedure is preferred for mastery tests, but it is difficult to illustrate here because of space limitations.

Set Standards of Performance

As noted in earlier chapters, setting standards of performance is easier for tests at the mastery level than at the developmental level. Where mastery is the goal, expected test performance can be described in terms of the percentage of test items a student must answer correctly to demonstrate mastery. The decision concerning what percentage-correct score properly indicates mastery, however, must be arbitrarily made. A standard of 80 to 85 per cent correct provides a good starting point. This can be increased or decreased by taking into account the nature of the objectives, the types of test items used, and the level of mastery needed for future learning.

For our illustrative unit on "weather maps," levels of mastery might be set for each objective as follows:

Objective	Level of Mastery
1. Knows basic terms	85%
2. Knows map symbols	100%
3. Knows specific facts	85%
4. Interprets weather maps	80%

In this illustration, knowledge of *all* map symbols was considered necessary, since the information is essential for map interpretation. The level of mastery for *Interprets weather maps* was set lower than that of the other objectives because the learning tasks are more difficult. These levels of mastery for each objective may, of course, need to be revised somewhat in light of our experience in teaching the unit. We shouldn't set performance standards in an arbitrary manner and then treat them as infallible.

Select the Item Types to Use

When the specifications for the test have been completed, we can turn our attention to the preparation of items for the test. The table of specifications indicates the number of test items to construct for each objective and each area of content, and the specific learning outcomes indicate the precise nature of the performance the student is to demonstrate. Thus, each test item should be designed to measure the behavior described in a particular learning outcome as directly as possible. Since different item types call forth different types of behavior, choosing the correct item form is important.

There are two major types of test items. (1) The *supply* type, which requires the student to provide his own answer, and (2) The *selection* type, which requires the student to choose the answer from among two or more alternatives. These two types are further subdivided as follows:

Supply Type:	Selection Type:
Short-answer	Multiple-Choice
Essay	True-False
	Matching

All of these item types can be classified as objective items (i.e., scorers can agree on the answer) except the essay. Since essay questions present special scoring problems and are of limited use in criterion-referenced mastery tests, we shall confine our discussion in this chapter to the use of objective-type items.

The following sample test items illustrate the four basic types of objective items and show how the items should be directly related to the performance tasks described in the specific learning outcomes. Note that each outcome indicates the behavior to be demonstrated and the test task calls forth that specific behavior.

SHORT-ANSWER ITEMS

Specific Learning Outcome: Writes a definition of each term.
    Directions: Write a one sentence definition of each of the following terms.
      1. Weather
      2. Humidity
      3. Occluded front

Specific Learning Outcome: Names the instrument used for measuring each weather element.
    1. The instrument used to measure the amount of precipitation in a given locality is called a (an) _____ .

Specific Learning Outcome: Lists the characteristics of a given weather phenomenon.
    1. List three main characteristics of a hurricane.

MULTIPLE-CHOICE ITEMS

Specific Learning Outcome: Identifies the units of measurement used in reporting each weather element on a weather map.
    1. United States weather maps indicate air pressure in
        A   inches
        B   feet
        C   pounds
     *D   milibars

TRUE-FALSE ITEMS

Specific Learning Outcome: Distinguishes between correct and incorrect procedures for determining each weather element.
   T F   1. Dew point is determined by cooling a sample of air until it is
    *   free of moisture.
   T F   2. Ceiling is determined by using balloons that rise at known rates.
  *

*Correct answers.

MATCHING ITEMS

Specific Learning Outcome: Matches each weather instrument to the weather element it measures.
    Directions: On the line to the left of each weather element in *Column A,* write the letter of the weather instrument in *Column B* that is used for measuring it. Each instrument in Column B may be used once, more than once, or not at all.

Column A	Column B
(B) 1. Air pressure	A Anemometer
(E) 2. Air temperature	B Barometer
(C) 3. Humidity	C Hygrometer
(A) 4. Wind velocity	D Rain gauge
	E Thermometer
	F Wine vane

These examples make clear the importance of selecting the item type that measures each learning outcome most directly. Thus, if we want students to "define," "name," or "describe" something, a short-answer item type is needed. Since these behaviors indicate that students should be able to supply the answer, a selection-type item would be inappropriate. On the other hand, if we expect students to "identify" something, "distinguish between" alternatives, or "match" things that are related in some way, then a selection-type item would be quite appropriate.

In deciding which selection-type item to use, a common practice is to use the multiple-choice item, if it will measure the learning outcome as directly as the other two types. The use of true-false items is typically restricted to those special instances where there are only two possible alternatives (e.g., distinguishing between fact and opinion, correct and incorrect procedures, etc.). The matching item is a specialized form of the multiple-choice item and should be used only where a series of homogeneous things are to be related (e.g., dates and events, authors and books, instruments and uses, etc.). The multiple-choice item is favored for most other selection-type test tasks because of its many desirable characteristics: (1) It can be designed to measure a variety of learning outcomes, ranging from simple to complex; (2) The use of four or five alternatives reduces the students' chances of guessing the correct answer; (3) The use of several plausible incorrect answers for each item provides diagnostic information concerning the most common errors and misunderstandings of low-scoring students. This type of diagnostic information is useful in planning remedial work for particular students and in evaluating and improving classroom instruction.

Write the Test Items

Each test item should be written on a 5x8 card. The specific learning outcome can be stated at the top of the card and the test item placed beneath it (like the examples in the preceding section). Writing each test item on a separate card provides for flexibility in assembling the test and in building a file of test items for future use. Placing the specific learning outcome at the top of the card makes it possible to file the items by instructional objective. It also simplifies relating the test item to a table of specifications when it is selected for reuse at some later date.

The specific rules for writing test items are too elaborate to include here. They are described in considerable detail in Chapter 5.

Assemble the Items into a Test

When a sufficient number of test items have been written for a test, the items should be reviewed and arranged into the final test form. The following steps provide guidelines for this phase of test construction.

1. Review the test items for relevance to the learning outcomes and for freedom from technical defects.
2. Check the set of test items as a whole to be certain that they match the table of specifications.
3. Group together all test items that measure the same instructional objective.
4. Arrange the test items from easy to difficult within the entire test and within each section of the test (to the extent possible).
5. Place the items on the page in such a way that they are easy to read and easy to score.
6. Number the test items in consecutive order.
7. Write clear directions for the test as a whole and for each separate item type.
8. Make duplicate copies (ditto or mimeograph) of the test that are legible and free of typographical errors.

It is especially important that items in a criterion-referenced test be arranged by instructional objective. This enables us to more easily score and interpret test performance in terms of each objective. Interpretation can be further facilitated by clearly labeling each section of the test. Thus, for our test on "weather maps," the first section would be entitled "Knowledge of Basic Terms" and all items designed to measure that objective would be grouped beneath the heading. The second section would be entitled "Knowledge of Map Symbols," and so on. The items within each section, and the sections themselves, would then be arranged in order of increasing difficulty, to the degree that such an arrangement is feasible.

As a minimum, the directions for the test should tell students how to record the answer and what to do about guessing. Since a correction for guessing is seldom defensible with classroom tests (Gronlund, 1971) students are typically told to answer every item. A minimum set of directions for multiple-choice items might read as follows:

> Read each item carefully and select the answer that best completes the statement or answers the question. Mark your choice by encircling the letter of the answer you select.
>
> Try to answer every item. Your score will be the number of items answered correctly.

More elaborate directions would include a statement concerning the purpose of the test and the amount of time allowed for completing it. Most teachers give this information orally, however, so it need not be included in the written directions for the test.

Provide for Test Interpretation

As noted earlier, student performance on a criterion-referenced *mastery* test is typically reported in terms of the percentage of items answered correctly for each objective. These "percentage-correct" scores are then compared to the required level of mastery for each objective to determine which objectives have been satisfactorily mastered. This information can be presented to the student on a simple report form like that shown in Figure 1. This need not be a separate form, of course. The same information could be added to the test blank itself, for use by the student when the test results are reviewed.

A similar report form could be used for tests at the *developmental* level, but here we would want to also include the student's relative standing in class on each objective. That is, how his performance on each objective compared with that of other students who took the test. This might be in terms of his simple ranking in the group or his percentile rank (per cent of the students getting a lower score). An illustrative report form of this type is presented in Figure 2.

Including both the percentage of items answered correctly and the percentile rank for each objective, enhances our interpretation of test performance. Note in Figure 2, for example, that this student consistently answered more than fifty per cent of the items correctly but that her relative standing was below average on the last three objectives. Thus, both the criterion-

---

Test Weather Maps			Student John Smith
Objective	Number Correct	Percentage Correct	Mastered (x)
1. Knows basic terms (14)*	12	86	x
2. Knows map symbols (14)	14	100	x
3. Knows specific facts (16)	12	75	
4. Interprets weather maps (16)	13	81	x

*Number of test items for each objective.

FIGURE 1. Report Form for Criterion-Referenced Mastery Test.

Test Biology		Student Mary Jones	
Objective	Number Correct	Percentage Correct	Percentile Rank
Understands concepts (20)*	15	75	62
Understands principles (20)	16	80	74
Applies principles (20)	13	65	33
Applies methods (20)	12	60	27
Evaluates experiments (20)	11	55	20

*Number of test items for each objective.

FIGURE 2. Report Form for Test at the Developmental Level.

referenced interpretation (percentage correct) and the norm-referenced interpretation (percentile rank) add unique and useful information to the description of test performance. See Clark (1972) for other sample report forms of this type.

Chapter 5

Writing Objective Test Items

The key to effective testing is to write test items that distinguish between those students who have achieved the learning outcomes being measured and those who have not. Nothing in the content or the structure of an item should prevent a knowledgeable student from responding correctly. By the same token, nothing in the content or the structure of an item should enable the nonachiever to obtain the correct answer. The ideal test item will enable the knowledgeable student, and *only* the knowledgeable student, to answer correctly. The following rules of item construction are intended to serve as guidelines for writing such items. More specific and detailed discussions of item writing may be found in measurement textbooks (Gronlund, 1968, 1971).

The illustrative test items presented in this chapter will be based on the weather unit used in the last chapter to illustrate test planning.

General Rules for Writing Objective Test Items

Writing good objective test items is an art that requires considerable practice. However, even the beginner can write items of fairly high quality by following a series of simple but important rules. Here we shall present the general rules of item writing and in the following sections the specific rules for each item type will be listed. Although these rules are applicable to both norm-referenced and criterion-referenced testing, they have special significance for the latter because here each test item is used as a *direct* measure of an important learning outcome.

1. **Write the test item so that it calls forth the specific behavior described in the learning outcome.** The process of preparing test items that are directly relevant to the specific learning outcomes to be measured is a matter of logical judgment. It consists of matching each test task to the performance task specified in the learning outcome and judging their comparability. The sample test items in the preceding chapter illustrate good agreement between test task and expected performance. Approaches using more systema-

tic procedures for relating test tasks to learning outcomes are being explored (Glaser and Nitko, 1971), but at this stage of development they have only limited application for classroom test construction.

2. **Write the test item so that the task to be performed is clear and definite.**   This is accomplished by carefully formulating the problem, expressing it in simple and direct language, and following the rules for correct punctuation and grammar.   Ambiguity is the bugaboo of objective test items and effective language usage is the antidote.   Each item should be so carefully phrased that the intent of the item is clear to the student.   We would not want a student to fail an item simply because he did not understand the type of performance he was expected to demonstrate.

3. **Write the test item so that it is free from nonfunctional material.** Typically a test item should contain only material that is directly relevant to the problem being presented.   To add material that is extraneous to the intended purpose of the item lengthens the item unduly, and in some cases may confuse the students or provide clues to the answer.   Note the wordiness of the following short-answer item.

> Weather reports are more accurate today because a number of instruments are used to measure the weather.   Name two of them.

This teacher wanted students to "name two instruments used to measure the weather."   Why not use this more concise statement?   The longer version simply increases the reading load and contributes nothing to the clarity of the problem.   In fact, some students might attempt to name two types of weather reports.

4. **Write the test item so that irrelevant factors do not prevent the students from responding correctly.**   A test item should be designed to call forth a particular type of performance.   In eliciting this performance, the influence of factors that are irrelevant to the main purpose of the item should be reduced as much as is feasible.   A test of achievement, for example, should keep the vocabulary and sentence structure as simple as possible to prevent reading ability from distorting the results.   Similarly, a test of arithmetic reasoning should keep the demands on computation skill low so that success and failure reflect differences in reasoning ability rather than differences in computational skill.   Responses to test items usually include more than one type of behavior. What we need to do is write test items that maximize the behavior described in the learning outcomes and minimize all other influences.

5. **Write the test item so that irrelevant clues do not lead the student to the correct answer.**   In concentrating on the preparation of test items that call forth the specific behavior described in the specific learning outcomes, irrelevant clues to the correct answer may be inadvertently introduced into the item.   Some of the more common types of clues are (1) grammatical inconsistencies that rule out some, or all, possible wrong answers, (2) verbal associations that make the correct answer obvious, (3) specific determiners, such as "sometimes" or "always," that increase the probability that a statement will be correct or incorrect, and (4) miscellaneous factors, such as

longer more detailed statements tending to be correct. Being aware of such clues makes it possible to avoid most of them during item writing. Asking a fellow teacher to review the items is also a useful method for detecting clues that might lead the nonachiever to the correct answer.

6. **Write the test item so that it does not provide clues to the answers of other items in the test.** Unless special care is taken during item writing, the material included in one item may provide an answer, or partial answer, to another item. This is most likely to happen where both supply and selection-type items are included in the same test. For example, a date or name called for in a short-answer question might be unintentionally included in the stem of a multiple-choice item. As with other types of clues, awareness of the problem and a review of the items before assembling them into a test is usually sufficient to avoid the error.

7. **Write the test item so that it is at the proper level of difficulty.** As noted earlier the difficulty of the test item depends on the type of test we are preparing. For a criterion-referenced *mastery* test the difficulty of the items is determined by the specific nature of the learning outcomes being measured. Typically, mastery level outcomes have a low level of difficulty and no attempt should be made to increase the difficulty simply to obtain a spread of scores. When preparing a test to measure degrees of achievement beyond mastery, however, a range of difficulty for each objective is desired. Here we need to construct items ranging from easy to difficult so that we can measure a student's degree of progress toward objectives that are never fully attainable. Thus, a range of item difficulty is not necessary for measuring the mastery of minimum essentials, but it is necessary for determining the maximum level of achievement that a student has attained.

8. **Write the test item so that the correct answer is one that experts would agree upon.** There is usually little difficulty in meeting this criterion when constructing items to measure knowledge of factual information. Questions of the who, what, when, where variety typically have one clearly correct answer. It is when we construct items at the understanding, application, and interpretation levels that special care is needed. Here, for example, we might expect students to indicate the "best" reason for an event, the "best" method to use, or the "best" interpretation to make. These are matters of judgment that require the answer to be clearly best and to be identified as such by expects in the area.

9. **Write the test item in positive form wherever possible.** There are three good reasons for stating an item in positive form. First, from a learning standpoint, it is usually desirable to emphasize the facts, concepts, and principles we want students to learn, rather than exceptions to them. Second, the fact that a student knows what is "*not* the case" provides no assurance that he knows what *is* the case. For example, he may know that "the approach of a cold front is *not* indicated by cirrus clouds" but not know the type of cloud that does indicate an approaching cold front. Third, the word "not" is frequently overlooked in test items and students respond as though the statement were positive. Thus, unless the learning outcome specifically calls for the identification of the exception, it is better to phrase the item in positive terms.

10. **Write enough test items to adequately sample the learning outcomes to be measured.** As noted earlier, the table of specification serves as a guide for item writing. The number of items needed to measure each objective and each area of content is indicated in the table. Where it is desired to interpret the test results in terms of each specific learning outcome, as well as each general objective, however, it will be necessary to include several test items for each specific learning outcome. This may, of course, necessitate expanding the table of specifications and lengthening the test. The main point to be emphasized, here, is that the test should contain a sufficient number of items for the types of interpretations to be made and the process of item writing provides an opportune time to make a final check on the adequacy of the test sample.

Constructing Short-Answer Items

The short-answer item may be written in question or completion form as follows:

> What is the name of the instrument used to measure the relative humidity of the air?   <u>(hygrometer)</u>
>
> The instrument used to measure the relative humidity of the air is called a (an)   <u>(hygrometer)</u>   .

The question form is usually more natural for elementary school students and is more likely to result in a clearly formulated problem. The completion form frequently can be stated more briefly, but special care is needed in the phrasing of the statement so that there is only one possible answer.

Short-answer items are primarily useful for measuring knowledge of factual information and skill in solving numerical problems. They are not well adapted to measuring at the understanding and application levels. Thus, they are more useful in criterion-referenced mastery tests than in tests designed for the developmental level.

In addition to the general rules for writing objective test items, there are some specific rules that apply to the short-answer item.

Rules for Writing Short-Answer Items

1. State the item so that the answer is limited to a number, word, or brief phrase.
2. State the item so that only one response is correct.
3. Make answer blanks equal in length (to prevent length as a clue).
4. Place answer blanks at the end of the statement.
5. For numerical answers, indicate the degree of precision expected (e.g., two decimal places).

Short-answer items are relatively easy to construct, but writing items that have only one correct response requires constant attention to the phrasing of the statements.

Constructing Multiple-Choice Items

The multiple-choice item consists of a *stem* that is stated in question or incomplete-statement form, and several possible answers. The possible answers are called *alternatives* and the incorrect alternatives are called *distracters*. Their function is to distract those students who have not achieved the specific learning outcome being measured by the item. The following items illustrate the use of stems stated in question form and incomplete-statement form:

Which one of the following instruments is most useful in forecasting weather?
  A. Anemometer
 *B. Barometer
  C. Hygrometer
  D. Thermometer
The Beaufort scale is used on weather maps to indicate
  A. air pressure
  B. air temperature
  C. precipitation
 *D. wind velocity

The stem of the item should present a clearly stated problem. This can be most easily obtained when the stem is in question form. A good practice for beginners is to start with a question and shift to an incomplete statement only when it will result in a more concise stem.

The multiple-choice item is useful for measuring learning outcomes at the knowledge, understanding and application levels. Because of its versatility, it is the most widely used of the objective-type items. Where the answer is to be selected, rather than supplied, one should typically start by writing multiple-choice items. A switch to another item type should be considered only where there is some advantage in doing so. For example, in instances where there are only two alternatives (e.g., up, down), changing to a true-false stem may be desirable. Similarly, where there is a homogeneous group of things to be related (e.g., map symbols and their names), changing to a matching exercise may be advantageous. Except for such special cases, however, the multiple-choice item should be used wherever selection-type items are appropriate for the learning outcome to be measured.

All of the general rules for writing objective test items, discussed earlier, apply to the multiple-choice item. In addition, there are some specific rules that serve as guidelines.

Rules for Writing Multiple-Choice Items

1. Write a stem that presents a single, definite problem.
2. Keep the reading level low (avoid wordiness and complex sentence structure).
3. If the stem calls for the exception, emphasize it (e.g., all of the following. . . EXCEPT).
4. Keep the alternatives brief (put all common wording in the stem of the item).

5. Make the alternatives similar in form and grammatically consistent with the stem.
6. Write distracters that are plausible to the nonachiever (use common errors and misconceptions).
7. Avoid clues to the correct answer (verbal associations, textbook language, length of alternatives, grammatical clues).
8. Put verbal answers in alphabetical order and numerical answers in numerical order.
9. Avoid the alternatives "none of the above" and "all of the above."
10. Review each completed item for clarity and for relevance to the specific learning outcome to be measured.

Where multiple-choice items are being designed to measure complex levels of achievement (understanding, application), some novelty is necessary. If the students are asked to identify an example of a principle, for instance, the examples should be ones that were not included in the instruction. Similarly, the applications they are asked to make should be to situations that are new to them. If students were asked to identify examples and make applications identical to those encountered in the instruction, their responses would reflect no more than the recall of past learning. Except for this added caution, the above rules for writing multiple-choice items apply to items designed for all levels of learning.

Constructing True-False Items

As noted earlier, the true-false item should be restricted to those situations that are limited to two alternatives. The following item illustrates this use:

T F When a cold front passes through an area, the wind direction changes.
*

It should be noted that there are relatively few situations, like this, where only two alternatives are possible (i.e., the wind changes or it doesn't). Even here, it might be better to switch to a multiple-choice item and ask students to identify the direction of the wind change. This would seem to be a more important outcome.

When a cold front passes, the wind direction usually changes from
A. east to west
B. north to south
*C. south to north
D. west to east

A major shortcoming of using true-false items, where there are more than two possible alternatives, resides in the fact that *false* items may be correctly marked on the basis of misinformation. Read the following item, for example:

> T   F   A wind of ten miles per hour is indicated by the Beaufort number 5.
>   *

Students may mark this item false without knowing that the correct Beaufort number is 3. In fact, the least knowledgeable student might think the correct Beaufort number is 10. He marks the item false and receives one point for his lack of knowledge. Of course, students who think the correct number is 1, 2, 4, 6, 7, 8, or 9 also mark it false and receive one point for their misinformation. In short, where there are numerous possibilities, marking a false item false provides no evidence that the student knows the correct answer. In this particular case, a short-answer item requiring students to supply the Beaufort number would be a better measure.

Even when the true-false item is restricted to situations where only two alternatives are possible, there are still factors that limit its usefulness in criterion-referenced tests. First, since students can answer fifty per cent of the items correctly by guessing, it is difficult to determine which specific learning outcomes have been satisfactorily mastered. Second, the item does not provide diagnostic information. The incorrect answers supplied on short-answer tests and the incorrect alternatives selected on multiple-choice tests, for example, both provide clues to the common errors and misconceptions of students. Third, the true-false item is limited to the measurement of relatively simple learning outcomes, such as knowledge of factual information.

If true-false items are used, special care is needed in writing clear, unambiguous statements. The following specific rules will aid in item writing.

Rules for Writing True-False Items
1. Write true-false items only where they are more appropriate than other item types (only two possible alternatives).
2. Write statements that can be unquestionably judged as true or false (avoid partly true statements).
3. Keep the reading level low (avoid vague terms and complex sentence structures).
4. Avoid negative statements (especially double negatives).
5. Avoid use of specific determiners (e.g., always, never, sometimes, may).
6. Keep the true and false statements approximately equal in length and number (to reduce correct guesses).

Because of its limitations, the true-false item might best be used for review and discussion purposes. It should be used for measuring student learning only in those rare instances where it is uniquely appropriate. That is, where there are only two possible alternatives and the item provides a direct measure of an important learning outcome (e.g., distinguishing between cause and effect, fact and opinion).

Constructing Matching Items

The matching item is a specialized form of the multiple-choice item. It is used where a series of multiple-choice items would have a common set of alternatives. In such cases it is more convenient to list the stems, or *premises*, in one column and the alternative *responses* in another. This, of course, makes it unnecessary to repeat the same alternatives over and over again for each stem. In the following item, note how the alternative responses in Column B could be placed under each statement in Column A to make five separate multiple-choice items.

Directions. On the line to the left of each statement in *Column A,* write the letter of the cloud name in *Column B* that fits it. Each cloud name in Column B may be used once, more than once, or not at all.

Column A		Column B
C	1. Low, gray colored clouds.	A. Cirrus
A	2. High, thin, feathery look- ing clouds.	B. Cumulus
		C. Stratus
B	3. Medium height, thick, fleecy looking clouds.	
B	4. Marks the approach of a cold front.	
A	5. Marks the approach of a warm front.	

The above item illustrates the important features of a good matching item. The material is homogeneous (types of clouds and their characteristics), the list of items to be matched is short and uneven (fewer responses), the brief responses are placed to the right (easy to scan), and the alternative responses are plausible for each premise (can be reused).

Since matching items are used to measure the ability to relate two things, they are limited to relatively simple learning outcomes. One typically starts with multiple-choice items and switches to the matching item only where it provides a more convenient means of measuring the same learning outcomes.

Rules for Writing Matching Items

1. Keep the material in the lists homogeneous.
2. Keep the lists relatively short.
3. Make the list of responses longer or shorter than the list of premises.
4. Place the brief responses on the right and in logical order (alphabetical or numerical).
5. Write directions indicating the basis for matching and that the responses may be used more than once.

As with the other item types, this brief list of rules merely supplements the list of general rules for constructing objective items.

Chapter 6

Using And Appraising
Criterion-Referenced Tests

As noted earlier, criterion-referenced testing is most effective when confined to relatively small units of instruction. This makes it possible to more clearly define the domain of behavior to be tested and to obtain a more adequate sample of student achievement. Testing student performance on each small unit of instruction, of course, requires devoting a considerable amount of time to testing. Since this takes time away from other instructional activities, the more frequent testing can be defended only if it contributes directly to the teaching-learning process. Thus, the testing must become an integral part of the instruction.

In this chapter we shall describe various ways that criterion-referenced tests might be used in the classroom instructional program and some methods for evaluating their effectiveness as measuring instruments.

Pretesting

Tests may be given at the beginning of a course or unit of instruction to serve any one of the following uses.

1. To measure prerequisite skills needed for the instruction (readiness).
2. To determine where a student should be placed in an instructional sequence (placement).
3. To determine what portion of an instructional area students have already mastered (curriculum modifications).
4. To provide a base for measuring learning gain during the instruction (pretest and posttest).

The criterion-referenced mastery test is especially well suited to serving most functions of pretesting because the results provide a description of the knowledge and skills possessed by the student. For most pretest purposes, we are not as interested in the relative ranking of students (norm-referenced testing) as we are in knowing what the students can and cannot do.   This enables us to provide any needed remedial instruction, to place students in the proper learning groups, and to modify the instruction to fit the students' strengths and weaknesses.

Where we desire to measure learning gain, our pretest might very well include items at both the mastery and developmental levels. If our posttest is designed to measure all of the learning outcomes of a course, for example, the pretest will need to have the same comprehensive coverage.

Formative Testing

The criterion-referenced mastery test is also well suited to formative testing. That is, to testing done during instruction where the primary aim is to improve student learning.   The following steps, modified from Bloom (1971), illustrate an effective procedure for using criterion-referenced mastery tests as an integral part of the instructional process.

1. Administer a criterion-referenced mastery test at the end of each unit of instruction.
2. Analyze the results to determine which objectives each student has mastered (see report form in Figure 1, page <u>32</u>).
3. Where an objective has not been mastered, examine the individual test items to identify the student's particular learning deficiencies.
4. Prescribe for each student the particular instructional materials and procedures he might use to correct his learning deficiencies (e.g., page references in the textbook, programmed materials, practice exercises, etc.).
5. Retest each student with another form of the test after he has had sufficient time to correct his learning deficiencies.
6. Use the information from the criterion-referenced testing to improve instruction (e.g., modification of methods, materials, or sequencing).

The above procedure assumes, of course, that each criterion-referenced mastery test is carefully developed following the steps outlined in Chapter 4. The procedure also assumes that the tests are to be used to improve learning and instruction and not to assign course grades. Since each student can be recycled through the material until he has mastered it, the assignment of course grades to the test results becomes meaningless.

Test items at the developmental level might also be included in unit tests, to determine what students have learned beyond the mastery of minimum essentials. Where this is done, these items should be placed in a separate section at the end of the test. Since complete mastery is not possible at the developmental level, the above procedure for testing and recycling is not fully applicable. Prescribing materials and procedures that will assist a student to improve his progress toward developmental objectives is, of course, both appropriate and desirable. It's just that it is infeasible to keep recycling him until he achieves the unattainable goal of mastery. If nonmastery standards have been set for the developmental objectives, these may, of course, be used as guides in the testing and recycling process.

Diagnostic Testing

The tests used for formative testing can also be used for diagnostic purposes if they are constructed with this use in mind. A diagnostic test is based on the common errors students make as well as on a representative sample of the tasks to be performed. A formative test designed to measure the addition of whole numbers, for example, should include a representative sample of the various number combinations. If the test is to serve diagnostic purposes as well, it should also include a graded series of problems that require no carrying, simple carrying and repeated carrying. Similarly, a diagnostic test of spelling should include words containing those letter combinations that contribute most frequently to spelling errors (e.g., *ie* and *ei*). Since a diagnostic test samples both learning outcomes and common errors, it tends to be longer than the typical formative test.

Summative Testing

A summative test is one given at the end of a course, or other period of instruction, and is used primarily for assigning course grades. Here we are concerned with a comprehensive evaluation of all learning outcomes, so test items at both the mastery and developmental levels are needed. It is usually desirable to arrange all mastery items by objective and place them in part one of the test. The items designed to measure at the developmental level should also be arranged by objective and then placed in part two of the test. This arrangement makes it possible to score and interpret each part of the test separately, by objective. The two report forms shown in Chapter 4, or some combination of them, can be used for reporting the test results to students. Other examples of report forms based on instructional objectives are presented in an earlier publication (Gronlund, 1970).

Where it is necessary to report test performance in terms of letter grades, these grades might be assigned as follows:

> A — Achieved all mastery objectives and *high* on developmental objectives.
> B — Achieved all mastery objectives and *low* on developmental objectives.
> C — Achieved all mastery objectives *only.*

This distribution of letter grades reflects the fact that students should be permitted to work on the mastery objectives until they have been achieved. The same recycling process that was used with formative testing can be used with the mastery section of the summative test. Thus, students are not failed. They are simply not assigned a grade until they have demonstrated mastery of the minimum essentials of the course. Where recycling is not possible, or not desired, letter grades of D and E can, of course, be assigned to students who have not mastered the minimum essentials.

TABLE V. A Portion of an Item-Response Chart for a
Criterion-Referenced Mastery Test on Weather Maps

Objectives →	Knows Basic Terms													
Content Areas →	Pressure		Temperature		Humidity		Wind		Clouds			Fronts		
Items →	1	2	3	4	5	6	7	8	9	10	11	12	13	14
John Able	+	+	+	+	+	+	+	+	−	−	−	+	−	−
Mary Baker	+	+	+	+	−	−	+	−	+	−	−	−	+	+
Henry Charles	+	−	+	+	+	+	−	+	−	−	+	+	−	+
Joe Darby	+	+	+	+	+	−	+	+	+	−	−	+	+	−
Betty Frank	+	+	+	+	+	+	+	+	+	−	+	−	+	−
Bill Jones	+	−	+	+	+	+	−	+	−	−	−	−	−	−
Louise Kerr	+	+	+	+	+	+	+	+	+	−	+	−	+	+
Kathy Mann	+	+	+	+	+	+	+	+	+	−	+	+	+	−
Douglas Smith	−	−	−	+	+	−	+	−	−	−	+	+	−	−
Frances Young	+	+	+	+	+	+	−	+	+	−	−	+	−	−

Analyzing Criterion-Referenced Tests

Before a criterion-referenced test is used it should be carefully reviewed
to be certain that it meets the criteria of a good test. The "Check List for
Evaluating a Test," presented in the Appendix, can serve as a guide for this
purpose.

After a criterion-referenced test has been administered to a classroom
group, an analysis of the results item-by-item can be useful. Such an analysis
aids in diagnosing the students' learning difficulties, in evaluating the effectiveness of the items, and in improving the instruction. A simple form of
item analysis is illustrated in Table V.

Note in Table V that the students' names are listed to the left and the
numbers of the test items are listed across the top of the table. The *plus*
signs indicate correct responses and the *minus* signs indicate incorrect responses. The performance of individual students can be determined by
looking at the rows in the table. The columns in the table indicate the
number of correct and incorrect responses for each item. The vertical lines
in the table group together those items measuring the same area of content
(air pressure, air temperature, etc.). This particular grouping of items is
based on the table of specifications in Table IV, Chapter 4. A complete

TABLE VI. A Portion of an Item-Response Chart Showing Correct (+) and
Incorrect (−) Responses Before and After Instruction

Items →	1		2		3		4		5	
Pretest (B) Posttest (A)	B	A	B	A	B	A	B	A	B	A
Jim Hart	−	+	+	+	−	−	+	−	−	+
Dora Larson	−	+	+	+	−	−	+	−	+	+
Lois Trent	−	+	+	+	−	−	+	−	−	+
Donna Voss	−	+	+	+	−	−	+	−	−	+
Dick Ward	−	+	+	+	−	−	+	−	+	+
Bob West	−	+	+	+	−	−	+	−	−	−

item-response chart would, of course, include a larger number of students
and would list the items for all of the objectives of the unit. The portion of
a chart presented in Table V is simply meant to illustrate the format.

The pattern of responses in Table V indicates that the majority of students
knew the terms in the first four areas of content but had difficulty with the
last two areas (clouds and fronts). In fact, enough items were missed in
these latter areas to suggest a general review. Before reviewing, however, it
would be wise to examine the individual test items for possible defects.
Item ten is especially suspicious, since no one responded correctly. It may
be defective or keyed incorrectly.

An examination of each individual student's pattern of responses in Table
V reveals two students in need of special help. Mary Baker needs help with
the last four content areas and Douglas Smith needs help with all of them.
Although an item response chart does not indicate the specific nature of an
individual's learning difficulty, it alerts us to the problem and indicates the
general areas of weakness.

A more comprehensive item analysis can be made where the same test is
administered before and after a unit of instruction. When this is done, the
students' responses to each item on the pretest are compared with their
responses to the same items on the posttest. This procedure is especially
effective for evaluating the individual items in the test. A brief example of
this type of item-response chart is presented in Table VI. The results in the
table are deliberately distorted to illustrate several basic patterns of item
response.

Item one in Table VI illustrates the ideal item in a criterion-referenced
mastery test. All students answered the item incorrectly before instruction
and correctly after instruction, indicating that both the item and the instruction were effective. Item two represents an item that was too easy and item
three represents an item that was too difficult. Since neither item type
measures the achievement resulting from instruction, we need to either revise
the items, revise the instruction, or both. Items like item four can be ex-

pected to occur infrequently, but they obviously indicate defective items or poor instruction. Item five illustrates a more normal response pattern for effective test items. That is, some students can be expected to respond correctly on the pretest but a larger proportion of the students will respond correctly after instruction.

The traditional methods of item analysis, developed for use with norm-referenced tests, require variability in the test scores. Thus, they are appropriate for tests at the *developmental* level, where a range of scores is expected. They are inappropriate for criterion-referenced mastery tests, however, because here variability in test scores is not relevant. Ideally, we would like all students to obtain perfect scores on a mastery test at the end of instruction. The problems of obtaining indices of item adequacy for criterion-referenced mastery tests, and some possible solutions, have been discussed in considerable detail by Popham (1971).

The Validity of Criterion-Referenced Tests

During the construction and use of criterion-referenced tests, we are concerned primarily with *content* validity. That is, with the extent to which our test items have adequately sampled the objectives and the subject-matter content of the instructional unit. The steps in test planning, outlined in Chapter 4, serve as guidelines for preparing tests that are content valid. The list of instructional objectives and the content outline define the domain of behavior to be measured, and the table of specifications clarifies the nature of the test sample. If test items are then carefully prepared in accordance with the test specifications, the students' responses should provide valid indicators of achievement. Thus, content validity is largely a matter of judgment. We must judge the relevance and the adequacy of the sample of test tasks for measuring the expected learning outcomes of the instruction.

Although content validity is our major concern with criterion-referenced interpretations of test results, we might also be interested in predicting a student's chances of succeeding in some future activity. We might, for example, like to know whether a student is likely to master the material by the end of the unit or obtain a passing grade at the end of the course. The extent to which test results are accurate in predicting some future performance falls within the province of *criterion-related* validity and can be most clearly expressed by means of an expectancy table.

An expectancy table is a two-fold table that places the test scores down the left side and the criterion-scores (measures of success) across the top. An illustrative table, for predicting mastery at the end of an instructional unit, is shown in Table VII. Note that all three students scoring above 40 on the pretest attained mastery and that only one of the ten students scoring 20, or lower, were able to attain mastery. Although these results are based on only 30 students, they do suggest that future students scoring 20 or lower on the pretest are likely to fall short of mastery unless they are given special help.

Another illustrative expectancy table is presented in Table VIII. This table

TABLE VII. Expectancy Table Showing the Relation Between Pretest Scores and the Number of Students Attaining Mastery at the End of the Unit (N=30)

	Number of Students	
Pretest Scores	*Nonmastery*	*Mastery*
41–50	0	3
31–40	1	6
21–30	2	8
11–20	7	1
1–10	2	0

TABLE VIII. Expectancy Table Showing the Relation Between Arithmetic Pretest Scores and Algebra Grades (N=220)

Pretest Scores	*Percentage Receiving Each Grade*				
	E	*D*	*C*	*B*	*A*
51–60			7	26	67
41–50		3	10	32	55
31–40	15	25	30	20	10
21–30	23	32	30	15	
11–20	50	30	20		

illustrates the use of pretest scores in arithmetic for predicting success in ninth-grade algebra. In this case the final grades received at the end of the algebra course serve as the criterion of success. The table was constructed by tallying the number of students at each score level who had earned each letter grade. These numbers were then converted to per cents. Although these per cents refer to what students did in the past, they can be used to predict what students are likely to do in the future. Thus, we can enter the table with any student's score on the pretest and, by going across that row, determine his chances for attaining each letter grade. For example, a student with a score of 52 would have 67 chances out of 100 of receiving an A, while a student with a score of 36 would have only 10 chances out of 100 of receiving an A. The probability of earning each of the other letter grades is read in a similar manner.

It should be noted that an expectancy table provides *criterion-referenced predictions* of future success. There is no need for norms. For any particular test score, we can make straightforward predictions concerning the probability of success on some future activity. Where the likelihood of success appears slim, we can, of course, take corrective action. In the case of our pretest in algebra, for example, low-scoring students might be placed in a general mathematics course or be given special remedial work. From a validity standpoint, we are interested in how well our test scores predict future success. From a teaching standpoint, however, we are primarily interested in how we might upset the predictions of low performance.

Statistical Measures of Validity and Reliability

Statistical measures of validity and reliability are typically expressed by means of correlation coefficients. These measures require variability in the test scores. Since score variability need not be present in the scores of criterion-referenced *mastery* tests (e.g., where all get perfect scores), such statistical measures are inappropriate (Popham and Husek, 1971). Although attempts are being made to develop new statistics for estimating the validity and reliability of criterion-referenced mastery tests, a satisfactory solution has not yet been achieved.

The validity and reliability of criterion-referenced *mastery* tests for use in classroom instruction can be best assured by careful test preparation. That is, by following the previously outlined steps to obtain content validity and by using a sufficiently large number of test items for each learning outcome to obtain dependable results. Where interpretations must be based on small numbers of items (say less than 10) we should make only highly tentative judgments and seek confirmation through other measures and through classroom observation.

Testing at the *developmental* level does lend itself to statistical measures of validity and reliability, since here variability in test scores in expected. The traditional procedures described in standard measurement books are appropriate for use with these tests (see Gronlund, 1971).

Cautions in Using Criterion-Referenced Tests

Although teachers have used elements of criterion-referenced testing for many years (e.g., percentage-correct score), the use of such tests to measure carefully selected samples of clearly defined learning outcomes is relatively new. Since there is little theory or research to guide the practitioner, the problems of adequately defining a domain of behavior, of obtaining a representative sample of learning outcomes, and of constructing relevant test items can be dealt with in only an approximate manner. Similarly, until a more adequate basis for determining standards becomes available, the setting of standards of performance must depend largely on the arbitrary judgment of the teacher. To use criterion-referenced testing effectively, at this stage of development, requires a recognition of the fact that it is a bootstraps type of operation. That is, we make tentative judgments concerning instructional objectives, test items, and performance standards, and revise and refine these judgments as experience and new information dictates.

The following cautions should aid in avoiding some of the more common pitfalls of criterion-referenced testing.

1. Do not reduce all teaching and testing to the mastery level. If this is done, the more complex learning outcomes are apt to be neglected.
2. Avoid overemphasis of those learning outcomes that are easy to identify and define. Educational importance should be the major criterion in selecting outcomes to be tested.
3. In setting standards of performance, keep in mind that future learning experiences are especially relevant. Learning that is *not* used is soon forgotten and learning that *is* used is reinforced.
4. When retesting students for mastery do not retest them on missed items only, as this directs their learning toward the particular sample of tasks. Also, if selection-type items are used, a proportion of the correct answers on the test can be accounted for by guessing. Retest with a second form of the test.
5. Do not give criterion-referenced tests to students for study purposes nor teach *directly* for the test. A test is almost always a sample of tasks and students should not be encouraged to learn the sample of tasks only.
6. Interpret criterion-referenced test results cautiously. If a number of students fail to master an objective, the fault may reside in the instruction, the test items, the standard of mastery, or the objective itself. Since these are all matters of judgment, none of them is infallible.

Criterion-referenced mastery tests can make a significant contribution to the teaching-learning process if carefully prepared and used with discretion. Likewise, criterion-referenced interpretations of test performance at the developmental level can provide a useful adjunct to norm-referenced interpretations. What we need now is more theory and research to guide us. Until this is forthcoming, we should proceed with caution and fully recognize the tentative nature of our judgments.

Appendix A

Check List For Evaluating
A Criterion-Referenced Test

Criterion-referenced measurement refers to the method of interpreting the test results rather than to the construction of the test. However, if a test is constructed to maximize criterion-referenced interpretations, the results will provide more adequate descriptions of student performance. The following check list was designed to evaluate the adequacy of a test that was specifically prepared for criterion-referenced use. Although most of the questions would be useful for evaluating any classroom test, positive answers are especially crucial for criterion-referenced testing. A negative answer indicates an error in construction that should be corrected before the test is administered.

An earlier publication provides a check list for evaluating a final list of instructional objectives (Gronlund, 1970). Since clearly defined instructional objectives are vital to criterion-referenced testing, that check list should also be consulted.

CHECK LIST

	Yes	No
Adequacy of the Test Plan		
1. Does the test plan include a detailed description of the instructional objectives and the content to be measured?	⎯⎯	⎯⎯
2. Does the table of specifications clearly indicate the relative emphasis to be given to each objective and each area of content?	⎯⎯	⎯⎯
3. Is the standard of performance reasonable for the learning outcomes to be measured?	⎯⎯	⎯⎯
Adequacy of the Test Items		
4. Are the types of test items appropriate for the learning outcomes to be measured?	⎯⎯	⎯⎯
5. Do the test items measure an adequate sample of student performance for each type of interpretation to be made?	⎯⎯	⎯⎯

	Yes	No
6. Do the test items present clear and definite tasks to be performed?	___	___
7. Are the test items free from nonfunctional material?	___	___
8. Are the test items of appropriate difficulty for the learning outcomes to be measured?	___	___
9. Are the test items free from technical defects (clues, ambiguity, inappropriate reading level)?	___	___
10. Is the answer to each test item one that experts would agree upon?	___	___
11. Are the items of each type in harmony with the rules for constructing that item type?	___	___

Adequacy of the Test Format

	Yes	No
12. Are the test items that measure the same instructional objective grouped together in the test?	___	___
13. Are the test items arranged in order of increasing difficulty within each section of the test and within the test as a whole (to the extent possible)?	___	___
14. Does the item layout on the page contribute to ease of reading and ease of scoring?	___	___
15. Are the test items numbered in consecutive order?	___	___
16. Are specific, clear directions provided for each section of the test and for the test as a whole?	___	___

Appendix B

References

Block, J. H. (ed.). *Mastery Learning: Theory and Practice*. New York: Holt, Rinehart and Winston, 1971.

Bloom, B. S. "Mastery Learning," Chapter 4 in J. H. Block (ed.), *Mastery Learning: Theory and Practice*. New York: Holt, Rinehart and Winston, 1971.

Carroll, J. B. "Problems of Measurement Related to the Concept of Learning for Mastery," Chapter 3 in J. H. Block (ed.), *Mastery Learning: Theory and Practice*. New York: Holt, Rinehart and Winston, 1971.

Clark, D. C. *Using Instructional Objectives in Teaching*. Glenview, Illinois: Scott, Foresman and Fompany, 1972.

Glaser, R. "Instructional Technology and the Measurement of Learning Outcomes," Chapter 1 in W. J. Popham (ed.), *Criterion-Referenced Measurement*. Englewood Cliffs, N.J.: Educational Technology Publications, 1971.

Glaser R., and A. Nitko. "Measurement in Learning and Instruction," Chapter 17 in R. L. Thorndike (ed.), *Educational Measurement*. Washington, D.C.: American Council on Education, 1971.

Gronlund, N. E. *Constructing Achievement Tests*. Englewood Cliffs, N.J.: Prentice-Hall, 1968.

————*Stating Behavioral Objectives for Classroom Instruction*. New York: Macmillan, 1970.

————*Measurement and Evaluation in Teaching*. 2nd ed., New York: Macmillan, 1971

Popham, W. J., "Indices of Adequacy for Criterion-Referenced Test Items," Chapter 6 in W. J. Popham (ed.), *Criterion-Referenced Measurement*. Englewood Cliffs, N.J.: Educational Technology Publications, 1971.

Popham, W. J. and T. R. Husek. "Implications of Criterion-Referenced Measurement," Chapter 2 in W. J. Popham (ed.), *Criterion-Referenced Measurement*. Englewood Cliffs, N.J.: Educational Technology Publications, 1971.

Scriven, M. "The Methodology of Evaluation," in Perspectives of Curriculum Evaluation, AERA Monograph Series on Curriculum Evaluation, No. 1. Chicago: Rand McNally, 1967.

Index